The Mansion of Happiness

THE

POETRY
SERIES

The Mansion of Happiness

POEMS BY ROBIN EKISS

The University of Georgia Press
Athens & London

Published by the University of Georgia Press

Athens, Georgia 30602

www.ugapress.org

© 2009 by Robin Ekiss

All rights reserved

Designed by Walton Harris

Set in 10.5/15 Scala

Printed and bound by Thomson-Shore

The paper in this book meets the guidelines for
permanence and durability of the Committee on
Production Guidelines for Book Longevity of the
Council on Library Resources.

Printed in the United States of America

13   12   11   10   09   P   5   4   3   2   1

Library of Congress Cataloging-in-Publication Data

Ekiss, Robin, 1969–

The Mansion of Happiness : poems / by Robin Ekiss.

    p.   cm. — (The VQR poetry series)

Includes bibliographical references.

ISBN-13: 978-0-8203-3408-0 (pbk. : alk. paper)

ISBN-10: 0-8203-3408-1 (pbk. : alk. paper)

I. Title.

PS3605.K57 M36 2009

811'.6—dc22   2009022174

British Library Cataloging-in-Publication Data available

for Keith

Oh! the small afflictions
In the hearts of toys!
. . . .
Oh! cemetery of Childhood,
Reveal your secret light.

—Joaquim Cardozo (translated by Elizabeth Bishop)

Contents

Acknowledgments   *xi*

ONE

Preface   *3*

First Birthday   *5*

Dark Girl Dressed in Blue   *6*

Genealogy   *7*

The Opposite of the Body   *8*

Eight Views of the Hôtel-Dieu   *9*

Mozart's Mother's Bones   *11*

The Question of My Mother   *13*

Meanwhile under the shade palms   *14*

The Bird of God   *17*

World without Birds   *18*

Elegy for My Father, Not Yet Dead   *20*

The Past Is Another Country   *21*

TWO

The Bones of August   *25*

THREE

A Brief History of Happiness   *41*

Conversation with Doll   *43*

Edison in Love   *44*

At the Doll Hospital   45

The Mansion of Happiness

    i. Walking, Talking Doll with Flirting Eyes   46

    ii. Alphabet Girl   48

    iii. What's Possible   49

    iv. The Game   50

    v. Morphineuse   51

    vi. Elephant   52

    vii. Elocution   54

    viii. Still Life with Fruit   55

    ix. Famous Ventriloquist   57

    x. The Dollhouse   59

    xi. The Toymaker's Daughter Recovers   60

    xii. Lamentation   61

FOUR

Android Clarinetist   65

Wunderkabinette   67

The Book of Dreams   69

Portrait of Houdini with Wife   70

The Lady Vanishes   72

The Voluptuous Dancing Girls of Egypt   74

What Makes Men Great   75

Hitler's Bath   76

Ships in Bottles   78

Vanitas Mundi   80

Notes   83

Acknowledgments

Many thanks to the editors of the following journals, in which some of these poems first appeared, sometimes in different forms:

AGNI: "Android Clarinetist," "What Makes Men Great"

American Poetry Review: "Preface," "The Bird of God"

Atlantic Monthly: "The Voluptuous Dancing Girls of Egypt"

Black Warrior Review: "The Bones of August"

Blackbird: "Meanwhile under the shade palms," "The Lady Vanishes"

Borderlands: "A Brief History of Happiness," "The Opposite of the Body"

Columbia: A Journal of Literature & Art: "The Toymaker's Daughter Recovers"

Epoch: "The Mansion of Happiness"

Gettysburg Review: "Eight Views of the Hôtel-Dieu"

Gulf Coast: "Portrait of Houdini with Wife"

Kenyon Review: "Genealogy"

New England Review: "The Past Is Another Country," "Dark Girl Dressed in Blue"

Poetry: "Edison in Love," "Wunderkabinette," "The Question of My Mother"

TriQuarterly: "Elegy for My Father, Not Yet Dead," "Ships in Bottles"

Virginia Quarterly Review: "Vanitas Mundi," "Mozart's Mother's Bones"

Waccamaw: "First Birthday"

"Vanitas Mundi" also appeared in *Best New Poets 2007* (Samovar Press) and on *Poetry Daily*. "Edison in Love" was reprinted by Broadsided Press.

For their generous gifts of time and support that made completion of this manuscript possible, I'm deeply indebted to the Wallace Stegner Fellowship program at Stanford University and to the Rona Jaffe Foundation.

For crucial funding, residencies, and the privilege of community as I worked to finish the book, I'm also grateful to the University of California at Davis, Money for Women/Barbara Deming Memorial Fund, Inc., Dorothy Sargent Rosenberg Memorial Fund, the MacDowell Colony, Millay Colony for the Arts, Headlands Center for the Arts, and the Bread Loaf Writers' Conference.

This book would not have been possible without the friendship, faith, and feedback of my colleagues, many teachers, and friends. At the risk of omission, I owe special gratitude to Eavan Boland, Ken Fields, Simone Di Piero, Susan Borie Chambers, Thomas Heise, Aaron Baker, Jen Chang, David Roderick, Rebecca Black, Peter Campion, Monica Ferrell, Amaud Jamaul Johnson, Shara Lessley, Bruce Snider, Sara Michas-Martin, Glori Simmons, Malena Watrous, Maria Hummel, Ron Slate, G. C. Waldrep, and especially Gaby Calvocoressi and C. Dale Young.

Finally, I'd like to thank my family, who (though they continue to ask when my novel is coming out) never question my single-mindedness; Ted Genoways and the staffs at *VQR* and the University of Georgia Press, for believing in this work and shepherding it; and Keith, who turns all my red lights green.

The Mansion of Happiness

ONE

Preface

I was raised in the company of dolls.

My mother, the miniaturist,
made pies the size of thumbnails.

My father, the shadowboxer,
talked only to the dark.

No one here remembers
the love of a chair for its ottoman
or the privacy of a shut door.

Windows grieve in their sashes.
They burn with interior light,
like blood oranges.

Imagine: a dollhouse in every room —

in every room, another room,
in every girl, another girl

looking out a tiny window,
her face repeated on the glass.

As two who could not pretend
to love each other,
we stared through grief.

Pupil, *poupée*, little doll
orphaned by the iris of my eye:
what did you see, what did you see

but that other girl in me,

the door to whose post was nailed
the smallest coffin,

hiding the name of God inside
like rust in the mouth.

First Birthday

When I was born, there was no noise for him,
while she heard everything at once:

roil of water steaming the windows,
damper of milk rushing in to the ducts,

clockwork cry of each contraction,
again and again, the same frustration—

unable to feed itself or feel the illuminated touch
that makes us breathe or sigh.

When they lifted me out of her
body's blue kiln, swollen as a fistful

of walnuts, veined cord
clinging to my neck like wisteria,

doll drowned in a jar, my spine coiled
like a screw into her woodenness.

When she told him, was he angry?
Was she waiting for something to begin?

Dark Girl Dressed in Blue

Night comes on in the city: that's the time
of infinite sadness, the accidental marriage

of heat and air, when the bulbs of consolation
light the sidewalks. In the museum's tomb,

many stone doors remain unopened.
Does anyone here know "The Dark Girl

Dressed in Blue"? My mother used to sing it,
wearing her midnight shift and piano face.

Afterward, the Emperor of Light
walked her back to the wards with his hands

in his pockets, conducting their own heat.
In the marbled dark her gaze resembled

Egyptian vases with their side-eyed views:
not what they see, but what sees you.

Genealogy

Nested inside her like successive Russian dolls—
    how much I might love,
        how brown my eyes
  or this Roman nose

that migrates across my face. The smallest stamp
    of bees across the apron of a dog rose—
        how much room is there
  for impatient tendency?

Only my mother's mother's mother knows,
    so deep inside the drop of me
        it cannot be divulged.
  A clue: the spine is laddered

for an uphill climb. In a photograph
    her dress was lovely, littered as it was
        with red umbrellas,
  hair done up in a bun—

and in the next, she has none. Where is that place
    in all of human history
        she can leave her mark,
  if not on me?

The Opposite of the Body

Of the face in general, let me say it's a house
built by men and lived in by their dreams.

When you've been plucking eyes
out of the floorboards as long as I have,

you'll see this, just as you'd see
the patience it requires

to render an eyebrow, half an hour
and an understanding of architecture.

When you see your body,
think its opposite: not the bridge,

but its lighted face reflecting the water,
some other city as seen from a ship—

your forehead, once ponderous,
now light as umbrellas—

still not beautiful enough to make time stop.
The pleasure in being a woman's

knowing everything's borrowed
and can't be denied,

as when you take apart a clock,
there's always another inside.

Eight Views of the Hôtel-Dieu

i.

The hospital has many wings;
    it's hard to tell where the meat ends
and the butcher begins. Doctors feel clinical
    when they can't heal.

ii.

Straight as the barrel of her intention,
    round as the stones where cholera resided,
the House of Crickets on the Rue de Scissors—
        before the boulevards, they spoke of it.

iii.

The Bird Market enters the window;
    bad news never comes through the door.
A room is a cage without feathers:
        a rational plan, like a garden.

iv.

The nurses are nursing their gargoyles,
    bathing their patients in steam.
Unbelievable Shoes, said the storefront
        she passed as she walked to the Opéra.

v.

False fronts line the way to the Opéra;
    the houses are gutted but clean.
Corinthian maid in her toga;
      the floors to be polished, need water.

vi.

Nothing lives in a house without people.
    That it gives off an aura of welcome.
The names of the streets are important;
        her husband won't visit without them.

vii.

Repeat this to muffle the moonlight
    that enters the window she's broken.
The invalid's dreams lay beside her;
      all night they lay sleeping together.

viii.

Whenever he loved her, he said so;
    it wasn't as if she was hungry.
The fish without scales was for supper.
      The bread was no harder than stone.

Mozart's Mother's Bones

Every shadow carries its own
        but is too dark to see it—
as in the nautilus
           each turn of light
    leads into darkness,

or the hall outside her bedroom,
        where we fought like children
about the disposition
          of her possessions,
    anger envelops love.

Recalcitrant as opals,
        Mozart's mother's bones
are buried in the walls
          of the Paris catacombs—
    hers lay starched in the sheets.

It was harder to make her love me
        than to drive the stars
into the ocean. I remember
          the wave cuneiform
    of her hair,

ridged like sand above her shoulders,
        and in the rain,
how she looked down
          through the pavement—
    something to do

with shame and disengagement.
          Love embraces anger,
somewhere other than where we've been —
               light piercing the dark
          shade of remembrance.

Mozart's Mother's Bones are buried
          in the walls
of the Paris catacombs. How else is there
               to bury this
          white, desirable death?

The Question of My Mother

The question of my mother is on the table.
The dark box of her mind is also there,
the garden of everywhere
we used to walk together.

Among the things the body doesn't know,
it is the dark box I return to most:
fallopian city ingrained in memory,
ghost-orchid egg in the arboretum,

hinged lid forever bending back and forth —
open to me, then closed
like the petals of the paper-white narcissus.
What would it take to make a city in me?

Dark arterial streets, neglected ovary
hard as an acorn hidden in its dark box
on the table: Mother, I am
out of my mind, spilling everywhere.

Meanwhile under the shade palms

the Turks are inside the egg
    on the backs of elephants.

It's customary to describe their attire:
    feathered headdresses

shedding quills in ribbons of heat,
    mustaches and slippers

curled fetal at the ends. Like everyone,
    they have their eccentricities:

one's reliance on his left knee,
    which implies a limp

he doesn't have;
    another's thumb-ring flask,

from which he drains
    a ruby-colored liquor.

Nothing happens inside the egg:
    the Turks are yoked to their carpets.

One might be missing an arm or a leg,
    admiring a pair of camels

drinking at a trough, the other spying
    on the lopsided love affair

of the Dowager Empress
 and the Raja of Ramnagar.

They don't know it yet, but he's to be
 assassinated by a hummingbird.

Meanwhile under the shade palms,
 I write, *this is not happening.*

Her egg is small, encrusted
 with diamonds. Death watches

through the emerald window.
 It moves against the shell,

through her body's dense waiting,
 up through the floor,

through the legs of the chair,
 through the skin-covered calves,

up through the arm
 in its pose of righteousness,

through the hand
 tethered to the wrist,

up through the golden barrel
 of the pistol, through

the empty tunnel
 of the hummingbird bullet—

out into nothing, into the nothing
beyond which there is

only the desert, white as the ocean,
white as the port of Tangiers

flooded with nightingales.
Because I write this,

they are singing to the egg,
and I am singing too.

That it might carry itself
to the precipice.

That the Turks might hear it
and brace themselves—

as they do— for a moment
just like this.

The Bird of God

Tutankhamen's ebony bed,
    made to withstand
five thousand years of nihilistic sand,
      didn't buckle under,

just as the bust of Sappho with one eye missing
    dutifully watches with the other
who comes and goes in the chamber,
      which incompetent heart does the kissing.

Needle descended from the sewing machine
    and typewriter
designed by the gun manufacturer,
      both rusted in their pinnings —

but not ice skates and the orrery,
    which still take their circuit
counterclockwise in an orbit
      around her most neglected library.

On the shelf next to tritus and whelks,
    a book called *The Bird of God* —
impossible to think an animal
      can live inside a shell. She used to

keep even the air around her still —
    how else to feed a sparrow from your hand?
She's no longer there, nor can any joy be found
      in that dead house, on that dark hill.

World without Birds

Songs of cagelings like goldfinch
    embalmed in wax—
what is it birds sing about anyway,

       their thimbled bodies
    flashed through with convulsions?

Do they stop warbling
    in the cornucopic ear
if happiness finds no currency here?

       Listen: a woman may be
    stretched in the intimate pose

of a penitent—
    but for how long?
Serenade of serinettes,

       white thrush of the throat,
    flush with invertebrate memory—

sometimes I am the daughter
    and sometimes the idea of her.
Even a man can't live in a world

       without birds. Chickadee:
what do you want from me?

Toothpick made from a humming-
    bird's claw? Razor strop,
breast pin, fossil?

        The blood of moths
    is on my hands.

Elegy for My Father, Not Yet Dead

after Adam Zagajewski

The smallest poppy seed in the world
still gets stuck in the teeth.

So it is with grief: if a fresco feels pain,
the wall knows it. Like a collector

who catalogs everything equitably,
I tried to love you— no distinction

between what's perfect and in sore need
of restoration— like the first film,

in which the train enters the station
and never leaves it for the blue blur of the future.

What obligation did Adam have to the apple,
or the beekeeper to the hive, for that matter—

who takes the honey and leaves the combs dry?
When I pass my dead father on the street,

will I say about him what Kierkegaard said
of Hegel: he reminds me of someone.

The Past Is Another Country

I'm no longer in love
with the sand that makes the pearl,

or anything grainy
that hardens its beauty

by passing through pain.
Bone revisits the porous soil

and presses itself into coal.
Whole colonies of canaries

refuse to return from *that* mine.
Is there anything yellower

than their dark shaft of regret?
The past is another country,

all its cities forbidden,
their borders closed to you

on every side, while here
God has many mansions,

all too small to live in.
When I inherit his palace,

I'll take my moat everywhere,
making difficult any crossing.

TWO

The Bones of August

i.

Not to go backward,
      not to watch the women
peddling in reverse past the church,

          the priest in his black habit
     receding from the chapel door.

Not to go backward,
      the bones of August
becoming the bones of March,

          branch of dogwood
     picked clean by frost.

Not to say *Yes*
      when asked the question
all women wait to hear,

          Are you anything
     like your mother?

Not to be photographed in her dress
      like a saint
carrying the instrument of her martyrdom,

          Agnes, and her tray
     of breasts —

or to throw the bouquet into the grave
        where Bartholomew hides
with his bloody knife.

          Not to burn
    half the house down—

and build half the house up.
        Not to forgive
the bad child

         when even the bad house
    is forgiven. Not to care,

not to carry the bones of August
        into September, foiled with redness
and nothing to squander

        but the buds of spring
    dormant in their boughs.

Not to ask, *Did you*
    love her? and leave
the answer in the ground,

        where everything difficult
  is buried.

ii.

Attend the dead,
        then welcome the bride—
backward, as Jews do,

            reading Hebrew,
        right to left.

First the mourning,
        then the celebration.
Backward, taking off

            the beautiful face
        of forgetting,

two names with the same face—
        all this time
a woman waiting inside me

            to marry.
        Invisible, impermanent,

windmill girl in her cage
        of breath,
insect girl in her element:

            impenetrable shell,
        putting on

the beautiful face of forgetting—
      Fury   *Sybil*   *Isis*
one of us

            wakes in her
       graveyard of guilt,

filamentary as fiber optics,
         one of us sleeps on
in the temple, lulled

           by the metronomic
       pulse of longing—

Did you love her? Are you anything?
       That other girl is dead.
That other girl is dead.

           What else can be said
       about that other girl?

iii.

Same as mine,
      skin of her hands
laid over the ivory bones,

          dark map
    of the body—   *Yes*—

it was dark,
      but I was darker
on the inside.

        When she was young,
    she was "a great beauty,"

in the same sense
      that "a roomful of adults"
is rarely ever.

        I was never
    like her, flattered

like a map
      under glass,
slender as an axle

        in a turbine—
    enigma relic:

feet of steel, legs of wood,
          cabinet of curiosity.
Even her reflection

          in a spoon
     was beautiful.

iv.

Labor into longing:
      wild enthusiasm
of the dynamo engine

           working in reverse —
   more power

in the leaf of a flower
      than the paw of a bear.
Is it necessary

         to remember
absolutely everything?

Golden hour on the birch-
      brailled bark,
weathered barn stacked

         with malignant logs,
  sweet mulch

of aether/ore
      in the morning air.
We hung drapes

        over the mirrors,
  they were flowered, too —

her bouquet a cabbage,
        assembled by a florist
from 120 roses.

          Incandescent light
     flattened their petals,

made lace of their thorns.
        Uncanny— nothing in nature
so rigid,

          nothing more harmful
     than her rare affection.

v.

August: honeymoon at Niagara,
     water shut off—
bad luck.

     Two bodies,
    a man's and a woman's

found face-
     down in the mud
at the bottom of the gorge.

     Neglected
   on the cliffs above,

Tesla's alternating current station,
     powerless
in its pure machinery,

     honeyed, lunar magnets
   waiting in their sockets

for the current to resume.
    Enough about friction:
this is about two bodies

     at the end of America,
  repelling each other

under the polar rush of water,
        generating their own distance
over time. Is it history

        or home
    that hurts us more?

Did she look into the gorge
        as into his face
    when she said *Yes*—

            to see the downpour,
        even when it was dammed?

vi.

Nothing in me wasted,
    a use for grief, even.
I wore it on my left hand.

        I was married to it.
    I planted myself

in the dirt:
    alphabets grew up
from the bones of my feet.

        I drowned my heart
    in the lake.

Black hole, such vanity—
    navigating the ear canals
like so many gondoliers

        trolling the watery streets
    looking for someone

to sing to. Beautiful
    fisherman who fished
my heart out of its lake—

        I did not die. I revived.
    I wore her face on my fingers

when I dug my joy
　　　up from the ground, singing:
Oh wooden coffin, woman's body,

　　　　　boulder at home
　　in its stone skin.

vii.

Yes, then, to all of it: to the drowned
      sea urchins, porcupine spined,
and the black-brain

         coral that sleeps
   on the ocean's floor,

ruinously blue. *Yes*
      to the vultures that roost
above the waterfall,

         that don't
   surrender their nests

at our dissolution,
      and to the bones that do.
To remember is to open

         one door
   after another

all along
      the white corridor,
to say *Yes* when asked,

        Are you anything?
   Did she love you?

To go forward
is to surrender
the necklace of tears she gave me —

this failed body
with my name on it.

THREE

A Brief History of Happiness

In the beginning, there was nothing—
        or rather,
nowhere else to start.

There was a girl buried
        in the dark silt
of her own heart, ribs picketed

like a fence. There was the private
        circumference of the yard,
a tree

with its poisoned crown
        of leaving. She kept returning
to climb it—

its fragrance was undeniable,
        the dangerous consequence
of every day lived this way.

It's just a muscle, she'd say,
        nothing compared
to walls or words.

There wasn't a prince,
        but there was a moon:
new, full, or quartered,

a house with many storied windows,
	incomplete encircling,
not knowing

when to return
	or what to return to.
Even nothing was some place

to start. Some machines,
	like memory, rewind —
others move forward

with mad knowledge,
	uncontrollable want:
there is no other kind.

Conversation with Doll

You cannot remember the face you met yesterday
without the clever engineering of the mind.

Don't feel bad: grief is also mechanical,
winding around everything we know.

I'm like that too— speaking only to myself
in the company of others. As they say:

wear the same dress every day,
rehearse your own forgiveness.

O sedentary life, more dangerous than a painting
of a woman bound by its frame,

showing her only face to the room.
Unable to look at anything

without a stone's sense of gravity,
I can still hold your body in one hand.

Edison in Love

Thomas Edison loved a doll
with a tiny phonograph inside
because he made her speak.

Is there any other reason
to love a woman? Did she say
the ghost of my conception

or something equally demure?
It's hard to be sure how he feels;
when he holds me, I fall apart.

I'm projecting here. He didn't feel
her first transgression
was in having no expression.

René Descartes, too, traveled alone
with a doll-in-a-box
he called his daughter. *Francine,*

Francine . . . is it better to be silent
and wait for everything
we were promised?

Or should we love them back,
the way a train loves its destination,
as if we have the machinery necessary for it?

At the Doll Hospital

All mouths are closed, except the cadaver's.
The surgeons have given up their hands.
Only the dead man's and his doctor's are intact.

The chief resident looks away, pathogen
of her judgment evident to everyone.
Some things she carries, and others she lays down.

Sad misfortune! Doll with its skull split in two.
Among so many eyes fixed in glass,
where will she find her tenderness?

She kisses the forehead of a fetus
preserved in spirits and kneels before insects
to bless them. Only lately

have they started to look entirely
like children— barefoot, sexless—
so she must hold them gently and pretend.

The Mansion of Happiness

At this Amusement each will find
A Moral fit to improve the Mind;
It gives to those their proper Due,
Who various Paths of Vice pursue:
And shows (while Vice Destruction brings)
That Good from every Virtue springs:
Be virtuous then and forward press
To gain the Seat of Happiness . . .
— Directions for playing the Mansion of Happiness

i. Walking, Talking Doll with Flirting Eyes

Above the door to the studio he'd hung a sign:
Vices of the blood are infallible.

His assistant brought in a tray, glass eyes
and bisque heads painted to look like mimes.

He chose one skull and gave it a mole
and lashes like my mother's.

Her inner bellows produced the queerest sounds,
as if she'd learned speech from the chirping

of mechanical birds. She could ask,
How many inhabitants in Paris?

when the brass wedge beat
the larynx string. In another room,

mother played her clavichord
while I practiced my infant alphabet—

then, bored, took up the doll,
which could always stand undressing.

ii. Alphabet Girl

Sounds are produced in the mouth,
    one letter at a time: *e*
requires a pendulum tongue,
       ah— protracted breath.

The iron lung hums
    under the power of magnets.
All day encased in glass
      in his lake of air

the tinplate oarsman stares forward.
    The teacher envies the infant
incubator, cylinder speech
      shaping the body

without words. *C* is for *clavichord*
    and *clavicle*, cello
mother in the corner
      adding consonant to vow.

Later in her room, her breath
    goes out like a candle—
articulate contraction,
         the long *oh* . . .

iii. What's Possible

There are ways to make a man smoke
or appear to blow bubbles.

A boy can raise a stick as if to scare a horse.
A woman can lift a hot iron to her cheek

to test its temperature. It's not hard
to articulate the tongue, its little boats

crossing the crumpled paper sea.
The moon on the water is made of leather,

light apprenticed to skin.
Inside the torso, wires connect

ligament to ornament, sinew to joist.
In this way, certain toys

are meant to be admired,
never touched.

iv. The Game

During the fever, Father circled relentlessly
with new toys. I could hear the perforated music
of his breath approaching, the insistence
of even his thinnest respiration in the room,
when he placed the boy on his velocipede
just outside the curtain
or wheeled a pram to the bedside
and lifted the doll in it to the window,
offering me its shadow. When I was lucid,
we'd play the Mansion of Happiness—
"Instructive, Moral, and Entertaining
Amusement"— his pawn always circling
the Seat of Expectation, mine
approaching the Summit of Dissipation . . .

v. Morphineuse

Certain circles of women take their injections together,
    including my mother
in her phantom skirt of Liberty silk,

delicate asbestos purse
    from which she pulls the bristling needle
and vial of syrup.

I'm there beside her
    when she leaves her body,
removing strand by strand a doll's hair.

I have to lift her skirt to see the levers,
    skin of her calves whiter than paper
embedded with light, pinpricked by the spire

like the air above a church,
    that blue rule of veins and cells
saying we're commingled.

vi. Elephant

Let's play Elephant, he said.
    You be the trunk
and I'll be the tail.

I was tired of knocking
    on Love's door
with my feet in the dust.

You be the water
    and I'll be the pail
was my only refrain.

What was hiding inside?
    The pacifier mushroom,
the dress that hems you in.

You have to empty it first
    like the streets at night,
hollowed out by everyone's fear.

Let's try this another way:
    You be the shell
and I'll be the snail.

There was no refraining.
    My legs snapped shut
as clothespins.

I couldn't wash it off,
    the blood-rust
circling the tub.

It's the dark's fault
    lovers can't see the moon
for all their mooning.

You be the pail
    and I'll be the water.
I stopped referring to myself

by the greedy *me.*
    You be the father
and I'll be the daughter.

For God's sake,
    if that door's bricked up—
try another.

vii. Elocution

There's life and how it should have been,
   each day's routine: toy duck pluming its feathers
silently in gaslight, modeling English —
     I slept in the yard. I felt the rain on my forehead.

I conjugated the verb 'to love': *he loved,*
   he was loving, he will be loved.
I practiced the exchange of nested vowels:
     imperative, transitive, locomotive.

Father dangled over like a watch fob,
   surrounding the bed with rails.
Trains whistled on the floor:
     cars disconnected from their tracks

don't forgive. The Pullman
   still rocks its mannequined berths.
The porter still catches his balance
     in the smallest doorway.

viii. Still Life with Fruit

Nothing echoes like grief
in the white knuckle of silence—

the closed fist of the pomegranate
and other things past ripeness.

The painting hung over his shoulder
like fog in the trees.

What was it he'd said before dinner?
Fingers sticky with apples attract bees.

Light lacquers the small fractures
in her face and the fruit on the table

in the classical vase. Laid to rest in her lap,
her hands never moved, except

when they ferried his plate
to its dishwater grave or slipped

a tiny mandarin from its sleeve of skin.
The berries had been soaked too long in water,

but in the painting, the grapes were sugared
on the vine, all that mattered

when the curtain of speech
rose between them, when he pulled apart

the sweet jeweled vowels
and took them into his mouth.

ix. Famous Ventriloquist

We weren't always or entirely alone.
   There were afternoon teas
with a woman from Tegernsee,
     and a famous ventriloquist who visited us.

I sat on her knee or his,
   pretending to speak German
by dropping my jaw. Father, too,
     was famously tight lipped.

He didn't try to stop me
   from looking down the dummy's throat,
glazed over with darkness
     like a night window.

He insisted the dummy wasn't
   a doll— but a body
with its water removed,
     the remains of a child,

its chest filled with chalk.
   The common discomfort of this talk
did not pass— it hung in the air
     above us like moths.

Even after explaining the thin treble
   in his voice, Father watched
the ventriloquist suspiciously.
     When Mother made her usual plea

that we finish this, her dead fingernails
   drummed the stem of a glass
and made no sound.
      No one but I saw her mouth move.

x. The Dollhouse

A glass of water sweats on a table,
a plate of palmiers snailed with sugar at its side.

A man leans against the mantle.
A woman sits in a chair, back pressed

up against its slats. A box of a bedroom
conjures an empty crib,

shadow of my father on the wall
when he stands at my shoulder and reaches in

to move the dolls around.
Every day spent with a doll

is a séance: who doesn't remember
the death of her mother,

or how she rose to the roof
in the palm of his hand?

The sheer wall falls away.
Nothing divides like imagination,

shut up in a dark room at night
when the children are done playing.

xi. The Toymaker's Daughter Recovers

The moon anchors the street when I wade out
past the fever. A paper owl sits on a branch
and asks, *Who?* The doll opens
and shuts her eyes and raises both arms.
The monkey nurse sits at the bedside
and swabs her forehead with a washcloth.
Two bears on the shelf enact a Victorian marriage,
legs just barely touching. The flywheel
that drives the tin peacock quietly works
its key-wind economy. The monkey nurse
feeds the monkey child in her lap
from an empty bottle. Below the window,
a wooden figure steps out from under an awning
and shields his head as if it were raining.

xii. Lamentation

My child of least resistance,
I am coming for you.

Through the grove of your good will,
I am coming for you.

As you sleep in the dust,
I am coming.

Dark-eyed pupil bent into the earth,
your sadness will not save you.

The consolations of memory
are beyond your reach.

Someday this will be beautiful,
little temple of forgiveness

whose golden doors
are too heavy to breach.

FOUR

Android Clarinetist

In that century before
    we entered the innermost atom,
they played games
    like Physionotrace:

assorted noses, eyes, and lips
    that could be placed
on the surfeit slate
    of a cutout face

and rearranged
    to form a Hottentot or Jew.
The question of race
    is still that inscrutable

God-in-a-box, back
    to the outermost Adam,
simple body siphoned
    like a water organ,

from whose subtle variations
    spring the complex
machine: trunk
    pulleyed by levers,

potato-headed predecessor.
    In the garden, he could choose
to grow or starve
    one flower

to force another
     to bloom— thus today
metamorphic industry,
          metaphoric as a bird

on the branch of a bare tree:
     curiosity, a kind of pain
consanguineous
          with conscience.

Is it sour or sweetness
     we desire
when we turn back
          to the code we've cracked,

as the Calvinists looked away
     from the Android Clarinetist,
physiognomy free
          from the defect

of imperfect individuality,
     not by any definition a man—
this kind of music
          wooden fingers make.

Wunderkabinette

A conch shell like a board game
      with its concentric conveyance
to the center,

          sweetbread tissue
   of the frontal lobe,

organ of civilization—
      so unlike His obsession
for the straight line:

          telephone pole
   and tree trunk,

ten-penny nail pried from the ark,
      and other instruments
of His invention—

          the only violin
   in Eden.

Caterpillar, understudy
      to the butterfly;
beetles

          pinned to linen,
   needle-thin antennae

outstretched from their concavities;
　　　　body hollow as an oven,
the abortive put up in a pickle —

　　　　　　eyes too big
　　　for its head.

More elegant proof of His intention:
　　　　the electric chair
is still a chair,

　　　　　　the mind that thought death
　　　could be made comfortable.

The Book of Dreams

Everything is inscribed: the paper hawk
and dried branches of statice,

topographic maps of the moon,
its face damaged by lakes,

the laundress bent over
the metal ribs of her washboard,

kettle on the cold stove,
generating more heat than an idea.

From far away, sound approaches.
Crickets rub their dry-wing blades together.

A child's first words sentence her:
I helped God make the stars.

Death hangs on the back of the door
and says nothing. Before it wakes,

the mind travels the usual route:
precipitous drop without a parachute.

Portrait of Houdini with Wife

The pleasure of contrast: not chained up
    in an oilcloth sack underwater,
holding his breath, but composing himself

for the camera, in his only suit.
    You have to understand photography—
unforgiving mirror, unlike oils that soften

the hard edges of a man's face
    if you want them to, or velvet curtain
shielding the pine box during an escape.

The audience imagines his bones contracting
    to a splinter. That's not at all how it's done—
the camera's lens blanketed by cloth

to keep it in the dark; any halo of light
    ruptures the film with shadow. His eyes already
turn inward to that place we're going.

She thinks about escape too:
    at the horse butcher, in line like the others,
or arguing over the price of bread

at the Market of Innocents. Adam's rib
    is forever hidden inside her chest
as the force of blows hibernates in a boxer's fist,

but she, at least, is smiling when he says,
    We have such a small family,
meaning *your body*

won't open to me— it's shackled
    inside its cage: love and rage,
whose bars are meant to be broken.

The Lady Vanishes

First, there's The Spirit Carpenter
    Drives the Nail of Conviction

with the Hammer of Truth,
    followed by The Animated Guitar—

fingerless music echoing
    like a stare in a hall of mirrors,

and Children of the Scissors,
    a daisy chain of faceless dolls

in trapezoidal dresses
    suspended in midair

like convicts on trapezes.
    Then I enter the box feet first—

a winter onion
    putting down shoots.

Many things do not exist
    for me: tree trunks

in their mulchy ascendance,
    photographs like paper mirrors

that have no choice
    but to remember a smile,

the inevitable approach of Love,
   which can't be diverted

like a train from its station,
   and impenetrable Beauty.

The face of a handsome woman
   isn't immune to a frown.

In the lobby, the trick mirror
   returns everyone's reflection

as a bouquet of flowers.
   Sawed in two, cloistered

by curtains, or some other way
   secreted from view,

then revealed: unlike
   the Fantastic Orange Tree

that bears fruit instantly,
   my sweetness won't ripen.

The Voluptuous Dancing Girls of Egypt

exhibited at the Paris Exposition, 1889

The Voluptuous Dancing Girls of Egypt
are seen in the streets of Cairo, dining
at the Romanian restaurant or visiting
Paraguay, across from the Medicine Pavilion,

with its harlequined maps of anatomy,
bread made with seawater for dyspeptics,
and twin exhibits: A Curious Case of Sweating
and Chest Development Due to Gymnastics.

At Machinery Hall, sympathetic ink
applies itself to a canvas of a winter scene.
Cobalt chloride sifted over the bushes,
when heated, turns the landscape green.

The Voluptuous Dancing Girls of Egypt
synchronize their watches at the Palace
of Industry, then take in the History
of Human Habitation— cave dwellers

capable of cultivating pineapples.
To return to the Hive of Memory,
they must wait their turn at the perfumery
and dab invisible vitriol on their wrists.

What Makes Men Great

Everyone knows the legend of Vaucanson's duck,
who could eat, snuffle, preen,
and muck about in mud,
though made entirely of wire and wood.

Without the shitting duck, Voltaire wrote,
what would remind us
of the glory of France?
Many great men make great mistakes,

as when von Kempelen's chess player
was revealed a hoax. Even Napoleon
lost his bid and crossed himself
when the mechanized voice declared *Checkmate*

from the Persian *schah mat*, the king is dead.
Ducked into the casket, under wooden arm
and never watching eye,
a succession of men

whose legs could be folded beneath them
like bird's wings, including a midget
who spoke only German
and flung himself from the frozen prow

of a ship. The fishermen who found him
said their dinghies were floating
far from the shore.
They had to wade out to meet him.

Hitler's Bath

Toes to tile outside the tub:
    not the old
Roman ritual hall

bisected by columns
    and frescoed walls,
or a ball-and-clawed foot,

gentle slope
    of a porcelain back
as Lee Miller leaned into it,

half submerged, half rising
    out of steam,
smoking arm

like a wooden spoon
    dragged from a boiling pot
into air, staring

into the lens of her
    husband's camera
with a no-tell look—

but the modern,
    walled sarcophagi
of a built-in: floor-to-ceiling

subway tiles, civilized
　　soap dish and pedestal
sink, squared off

by mirrored vanity
　　bearing the classical
torso of a nude.

A man who slaughters
　　bathes the same
as a man who saves.

What things men do
　　without conscience or care
can't keep history at bay there

any more than the stop bath
　　fluid in which she floated
the photograph

to force its clarity
　　is moved
by the darkness

within the developing room,
　　current from which
only paper can be lifted.

Ships in Bottles

Somewhere inside is the sea,
        lapping against the transparent
wall of memory. Is it vanity

                that makes me see
        the imperfections in glass?

In a basement, under the hood
        of a lamp, a man
huddles over a schooner,

                rigging a tiny sail
        with tweezers. Upstairs,

his wife soaps a plate
        and stares out the window
at the yard

                where my mother,
        as a child, broke

the bottled ocean
        over her knee, acting out
the smallest gesture

                of anger. A window's
        for looking into

not out of— the pastness of the past
                isn't trapped in glass,
like some vast Lascauxan cave

                        on whose walls survive
            the outline of a deer,

or the wasp waist
            of a bottle's neck
through which a ship can pass

                        unstoppered, its mast
            folded to fit

through the narrow opening
            of a day.
I'm tired of writing

                        about the living as if
            they were already dead.

Let bygones be. Let me empty
            the typeface on the table,
above which ships

                        launch themselves
            into open air.

Vanitas Mundi

To make perfume from an iris,
    you have to mash the roots
but leave the petals intact:

as in *vanitas mundi*, skeletons
    are made of fruit and flowers,
not the dour bones.

It's this way with any form
    of pleading: *please* begins
with *plea*— linguistic insurgency

driven by a sense of urgency,
    not the sort of error in logic
a "war on terror" implies.

Hidden inside: the ornamental
    edge of understanding,
returned to us through language—

moving but rootless,
    like spent blood
circling the veins.

The consolation of physics
    is art: scoliotic curve
of the earth, cello

that was Adam's
   first knowledge
of women's pinched waists,

gland of a mussel that dyes
   the emperor's robes
imperial purple. Like hell

or hello, homonym
   or homophone, who prey
on each other's predicate,

what can we know
   of the world
but every measure of regret

carried in a word
   with the gravity of air:
begot, beget, begin.

Notes

One of the first board games published in the United States, the Mansion of Happiness was created by Anne Abbott, the daughter of a Massachusetts clergyman. Like many Victorian games, it was predicated on strict moral standards such as piety, honesty, prudence, and humility. First manufactured in 1843 by W. & S. B. Ives and reintroduced by Parker Brothers in 1894, it is the precursor to Milton Bradley's popular contemporary board game the Game of Life.

The Hôtel-Dieu in Paris is the oldest continually operating hospital in Europe, founded in the seventh century. In the 1880s it was affiliated with the Salpêtrière, the women's public asylum where hysteria was first diagnosed and treated.

The phrase "the past is another country" comes from Eugen Weber's sociological history *France, Fin de Siècle* (Cambridge, Mass.: Belknap Press, 1986).

In "The Bones of August," the phrase "welcome the bride . . . attend the dead" is loosely translated from the Hebrew prayer Eilu Devarim, read on Yom Kippur, the Day of Atonement. The phrase "More power in the leaf of a flower than the paw of a bear" is taken from the letters of Nikola Tesla.

In "The Voluptuous Dancing Girls of Egypt," details about the 1889 Paris Exposition were culled from pamphlets, maps of the fairgrounds, and catalogs of exhibits kindly provided by Mark Singer, reference librarian at the Mechanics' Institute Library in San Francisco.

In "What Makes Men Great," Vaucanson's duck refers to an automaton exhibited in Paris in 1738. Baron Wolfgang von Kempelen's Turk, introduced in Vienna in 1770, was a chess-playing automaton famous for defeating Benjamin Franklin, Napoleon, and Catherine the Great, among others. Though debates ensued about the Turk's ability to reason, it was later revealed a hoax; a hidden cabinet beneath the figure concealed a rotating fellowship of accomplished chess masters, all of whom kept von Kempelen's secret.

BOOKS IN THE SERIES

The History of Anonymity
Jennifer Chang

Hardscrabble
Kevin McFadden

Field Folly Snow
Cecily Parks

Boy
Patrick Phillips

Salvinia Molesta
Victoria Chang

Anna, Washing
Ted Genoways

Free Union
John Casteen

Quiver
Susan B. A. Somers-Willett

The Mansion of Happiness
Robin Ekiss

*Illustrating the Machine That Makes the World:
From J. G. Heck's 1851 Pictorial Archive of Nature and Science*
Joshua Poteat